Contents

Any words appearing in the text in bold,
like this, are explained in the glossary.

What are drugs?

A drug is any substance that affects your body and changes the way you feel. There are three groups of drugs – **medicines**, **legal drugs** and **illegal drugs**.

Medicines

Many medicines, such as cough medicines and painkillers, help to soothe the symptoms of a disease. Other medicines, such as antiseptic cream and antibiotics, tackle the disease itself. Some medicines can only be **prescribed** by doctors, but others can be bought from a chemist or supermarket.

Legal or illegal?

Legal drugs include medicines, of course, but the term usually refers to drugs such as alcohol and tobacco. These drugs affect the way a person feels but are not illegal for adults. Tea, coffee and cola are legal drugs too. Illegal drugs include **cannabis**, **heroin**, **Ecstasy** and **LSD** and are forbidden by law.

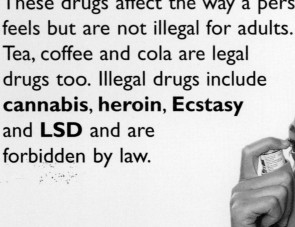

People who suffer from asthma sometimes need a medicine to help them to breathe more easily. The drug may be taken as a tablet or breathed in from a spray.

Learn to Say No!

Solvents

Angela Royston

Heinemann
LIBRARY

H www.heinemann.co.uk
Visit our website to find out more information about **Heinemann Library** books.

To order:
☎ Phone 44 (0) 1865 888066
📄 Send a fax to 44 (0) 1865 314091
💻 Visit the Heinemann Bookshop at www.heinemann.co.uk to browse our catalogue and order online.

First published in Great Britain by Heinemann Library,
Halley Court, Jordan Hill, Oxford OX2 8EJ
a division of Reed Educational and Professional Publishing Ltd.
Heinemann is a registered trademark of Reed Educational & Professional Publishing Ltd.

OXFORD MELBOURNE AUCKLAND
JOHANNESBURG BLANTYRE GABORONE
IBADAN PORTSMOUTH (NH) USA CHICAGO

Designed by AMR
Illustrations by Art Construction
Originated by Ambassador
Printed in Hong Kong/China

05 04 03 02 01
10 9 8 7 6 5 4 3 2 1

ISBN 0431 09908 1
This title is also available in a hardback library edition (ISBN 0 431 09903 0)

British Library Cataloguing in Publication Data
Royston, Angela
  Solvents. – (Learn to say no)
  1. Solvent abuse – Juvenile literature
  I. Title
  362.2'99

Acknowledgements
The Publishers would like to thank the following for permission to reproduce photographs:
Chris Honeywell, p.5; David Walker, pp.20, 23; Eye Ubiquitous, p.21; Gareth Boden, pp.4, 28; Image Bank, pp.13, 18; John Cleare, p.29; Magnum Photos, pp.14, 17; Popperfoto, p.8; Sally & Richard Greenhill, p.22; Telegraph Colour Library, p.19; Tony Stone, pp.6, 26, 27; Trip, p.25

Cover photograph reproduced with permission of Gareth Boden

Our thanks to John McVey & Warren Hawksley of Re-Solv for their comments in the preparation of this book.

Every effort has been made to contact copyright holders of any material reproduced in this book. Any omissions will be rectified in subsequent printings if notice is given to the Publisher.

Volatile substances

This book will tell you about sniffing solvents and other **volatile substances**. The substances that people sniff are everyday things, such as glue and lighter fuel. They are not drugs if they are used in the way they are intended, but when they are sniffed they become dangerous drugs.

Many drugs are legal, including the tea and coffee we drink every day.

Did you know?

When inhaled (breathed in) a solvent is a **hallucinogen**. A hallucinogen alters the way a person sees or hears things. Apart from medicines, most drugs are either **stimulants, depressants** or hallucinogens. A stimulant, such as caffeine in cola and coffee, makes your body work faster. A depressant, such as solvents and alcohol, slows the body down and makes the person relax.

What are solvents?

From liquid to vapour

A solvent is a liquid with another **chemical** dissolved in it. Many products such as nail varnish and paint are dissolved in solvents. They are sold as liquids in airtight containers. When the varnish or paint is applied, the solvent quickly **evaporates** into the air. This means that the liquid solvent becomes a **vapour** and the varnish or paint soon dries hard. **Volatile substances**, such as petrol and **butane** gas, also evaporate quickly.

Dangerous fumes

Substances that evaporate quickly can easily be **inhaled**. In some industries the workers wear masks to protect them from the **fumes**. The chemicals in the solvents can damage their lungs and affect their brain, making them feel 'drunk'. Some people like the way that inhaling solvents makes them feel. They deliberately breathe the vapour deep into their lungs. This is called '**sniffing**' or solvent abuse.

A professional painter uses a mask so that he does not breathe in the vapour from the paint spray. He knows the spray will damage his lungs if he breathes it in.

Aerosols

Many **aerosols** contain solvents, but they also contain another gas which can be inhaled. This is the gas that pushes the substance out of the can and it is called the **propellant**. It is very cold and particularly dangerous to inhale because it can freeze the throat and make the user choke.

All of these products have been used for sniffing. They contain liquids which are called solvents or volatile substances.

Solvents and the law

Police arrest

In Britain it is not against the law to have solvents or even to **inhale** them. However, although young people will not be **charged** for inhaling, they will be charged if they have committed a crime. For example, if the police see people being rowdy and abusive they can arrest them for causing a disturbance. In Scotland young people who are caught **sniffing** may be taken into the care of the local authorities. It is, of course, illegal for anyone to drive a vehicle or operate a machine when they are affected by any drug, including solvents.

Inhaling is not illegal, but sniffing can make people rowdy and aggressive. This policeman has stopped this boy because he thinks he might be in danger of hurting himself.

Imprisonment

In Australia and the United States the law varies from state to state. In Maine, for example, people who inhale **volatile substances** can be sent to prison for up to eleven months, while in Massachusetts they can be detained for 24 hours.

Illegal sales

In cases of solvent abuse, it is usually the shopkeeper who is breaking the law. In Britain, shopkeepers cannot sell lighter fuel to anyone under the age of 18. It is illegal for shopkeepers in most countries to sell solvents and similar products to people under 18 years old if they have a good idea that the products are going to be sniffed. So don't be surprised or upset if a shopkeeper refuses to sell you glue or other solvents.

The right to buy?

What would you do if a shopkeeper refused to sell you a substance, such as a glue or nail varnish, which contained solvents or volatile substances? Would you try to explain that you were not going to sniff it or would you accept that the shopkeeper is only doing his or her job?

Effects on the body

What happens when people sniff?

When someone breathes in gas from a solvent, the **fumes** pass through the nose into the throat and then down the breathing tubes into the lungs. The **chemicals** in the fumes pass into the blood and are pumped around the body. The chemicals take effect very quickly. They make the person feel **high** – dizzy and a bit drunk. They may also feel sick.

A lack of oxygen

Many of the effects of **sniffing**, such as dizziness and passing out, are due to a lack of oxygen in the body. Normally we breathe in air, which is a mixture of the gases oxygen and nitrogen. The oxygen passes into our blood and keeps all the body's **cells** alive. When someone **inhales** other chemicals, less oxygen gets into the body.

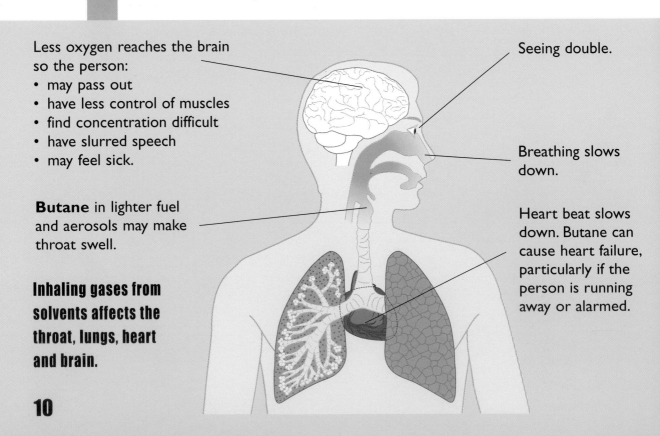

Less oxygen reaches the brain so the person:
- may pass out
- have less control of muscles
- find concentration difficult
- have slurred speech
- may feel sick.

Butane in lighter fuel and aerosols may make throat swell.

Inhaling gases from solvents affects the throat, lungs, heart and brain.

Seeing double.

Breathing slows down.

Heart beat slows down. Butane can cause heart failure, particularly if the person is running away or alarmed.

10

Inhaling from a plastic bag can be dangerous, particularly if the person puts their whole head into the bag. If they pass out, the bag may cling to their face and **suffocate** them.

The after effects

Most of the effects of sniffing do not last for more than about half an hour. However, after the chemicals have worn off, the person may have a hangover. They may feel moody and have a bad headache which will last for about a day. They will also find it difficult to concentrate.

People often inhale solvent out of a bag because the **fumes** are stronger and the effects are greater, but a bag can easily suffocate the sniffer.

Effects on the mind

Fooling about

Most people **inhale** solvents because it makes them feel light-headed and happy. They laugh a lot, even at things that are not really funny. They like to fool about and fall around.

Hidden dangers

Solvents affect the brain so that the person becomes confused and slower to react to ordinary dangers such as crossing a road. Their judgement is affected and they are more likely to have an accident and hurt themselves. Sniffing also makes people less inhibited or shy. This means that they are less able to control themselves. Some people shout loudly and become more aggressive when they have been **sniffing**.

Did you know?

About one in every eight deaths due to solvents are caused by accidents. The most common accidents are road accidents, drowning by falling in canals or lakes and falling from high buildings.

Talking point

Neil and his friends say that they inhale solvents because they are bored. They always go to a special place near a railway station. They like to hear the trains thundering close by because it adds to the feeling of danger. Why do you think people like Neil enjoy the feeling of danger? Do you think they are aware of the real dangers?

Hallucinations

About half of the people who sniff solvents say they do so because it makes them **hallucinate**. This means that things look unreal to them or they see things that they know are not really there. They may see cartoon monsters or feel as if they are flying. Sometimes a group of people share the same hallucination and this makes them feel close to each other. These hallucinations can be very frightening and may become like a terrifying horror film.

Many people like to sniff because it can make things seem distorted and unreal. This unreal world can sometimes become a nightmare.

Regular sniffing

An escape

People who **inhale** often have to take larger and larger amounts to get **high**. However, solvents are not **physically addictive**. This means that a solvent abuser does not need to inhale to feel normal. However, solvents can become **psychologically addictive**. People who use them are often bored and unhappy. They sniff solvents to help them escape from their problems. A few people feel that they cannot live without solvents.

Vandalism is often associated with solvent abuse.

Lasting damage

Although solvents damage the body, the damage is not usually permanent. As soon as the person stops sniffing, the body begins to repair itself. But some solvents can cause lasting damage. Inhaling **fumes** from **aerosols** and cleaning fluids for several years can damage the kidneys and liver permanently. Solvents such as leaded petrol and some paints contain lead which can cause lasting brain damage.

Unknown medical problems

A few people have an underlying medical problem which is made worse by solvent abuse. For example, they may have a weakness in their kidneys or heart which they are not aware of and which would normally not affect them. But regular **sniffing** can make the problem worse and cause serious illness.

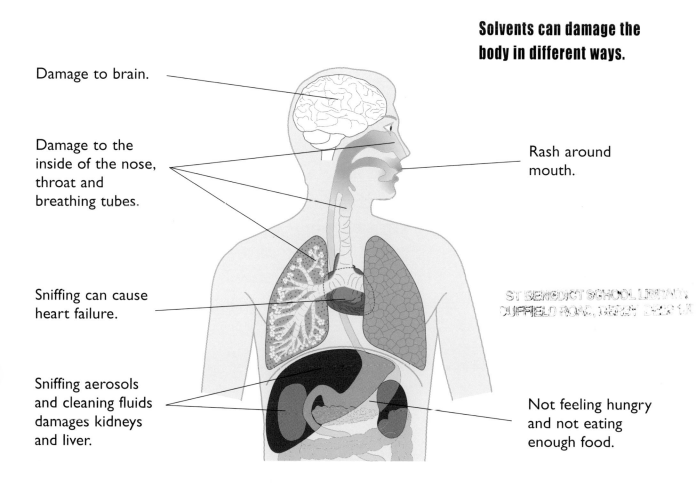

Solvents can damage the body in different ways.

Damage to brain.

Damage to the inside of the nose, throat and breathing tubes.

Sniffing can cause heart failure.

Sniffing aerosols and cleaning fluids damages kidneys and liver.

Rash around mouth.

Not feeling hungry and not eating enough food.

Did you know?

Sniffing leaded petrol causes brain damage. Many street children in South Africa cannot think or speak properly due to brain damage from solvent abuse. They cannot remember things or control their muscles properly.

Danger!

Deadly results

Inhaling solvents can kill you. The most dangerous way to **inhale** solvents is to spray an **aerosol** straight into the mouth and throat. Many aerosols and lighter fuels contain **butane** which makes the throat swell up. This means the person cannot then breathe. As a result, he or she **suffocates**. One of the biggest causes of death is heart attack. Aerosols and butane can make the heart particularly sensitive to shock and excitement.

Death by choking

Solvents can kill in other ways too. Many people pass out when they inhale. If they are inhaling from a large plastic bag, the bag can stick to their face and suffocate them. If they are sick when they are **unconscious**, the vomit gets stuck in their throat and chokes them, or they breathe some of the vomit into their lungs and drown.

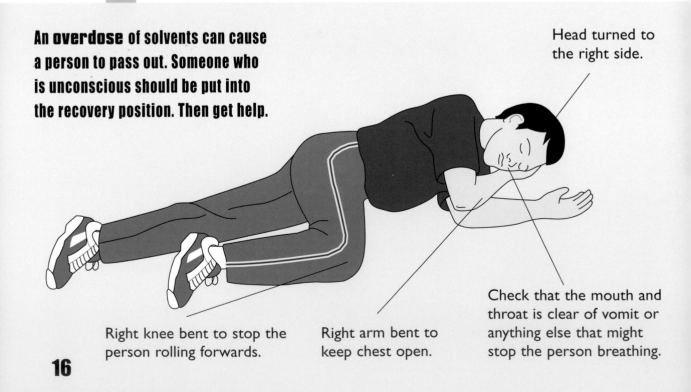

An **overdose** of solvents can cause a person to pass out. Someone who is unconscious should be put into the recovery position. Then get help.

Head turned to the right side.

Right knee bent to stop the person rolling forwards.

Right arm bent to keep chest open.

Check that the mouth and throat is clear of vomit or anything else that might stop the person breathing.

Other dangers

Most people who inhale solvents do not die, but they are still in danger. Users have little control over which **chemicals** they are inhaling and different people react to different amounts of chemicals. Some people become violent. Many users accidentally injure themselves or other people. Solvents burn easily. If someone spills solvent on their clothes and then lights a match, their clothes could catch fire.

People who abuse solvents often go to lonely places where they will not be noticed by the police or their parents. But this means that there is no one nearby to help them if things go wrong.

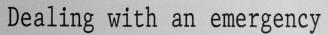

Dealing with an emergency

Would you know what to do if you found someone who was unconscious? Getting help is important but sometimes immediate help is needed. Do you think that schools should teach basic first aid, or do you think that the emergency services are the best people to cope with a crisis?

Why do some people do it?

Cheap 'highs'

Most people who use solvents do so because they think that they will like the way it makes them feel. They forget about the dangers. They think it will give them a 'buzz' and that it will be fun.

Some young people see adults getting drunk on alcohol and decide to do something similar. Solvents are cheaper than alcohol and the effects wear off much quicker. Solvents are easy to get hold of because so many everyday products contain them. Solvents may seem to be a cheap and easy way to get **high**.

Curiosity and boredom

Many people **inhale** for the first time out of curiosity. They want to see what it is like and they only do it once or twice. Other people inhale because they are bored and they can't think of anything else to do. If their friends are inhaling, they decide to try it too. Some people use solvents because they think it is daring and they like to shock other people. Many older people are alarmed and frightened by the way young people behave when they are high on solvents.

Young people who are lonely and bored may inhale solvents to become part of a group.

Inhaling alone

Some people inhale because they are very unhappy and want to escape from their problems. Inhaling alone is particularly dangerous because there is no one to help if anything goes wrong.

Did you know?

Of the few people who do try solvents, most give up almost straight away because it is so dangerous and unpleasant. About half inhale only once and most of the rest inhale only a few times. Only a tenth carry on sniffing for a few months and even fewer become regular abusers.

Over 100 million children in the world live on the street. Many of them inhale solvents. They often do it so that they can stay awake and alert to other dangers, such as street violence. Inhaling also stops them from feeling hungry.

Think about it

Stephen's father is out of work and often drunk and his mother is hardly ever at home. Stephen is bullied by his older brother. He inhales solvents to escape and have some fun, but inhaling soon gets him into trouble at school, so his problems increase. If Stephen was your friend what would you say to him? Where could he go for help?

19

Giving up

Giving up solvents can mean that you have to find new friends. Try to find a group of friends who accept you as you are and don't simply want you to be like them.

Most people who **inhale** solvents give up after trying it once or twice. Many people do not like the way the **chemicals** make them feel. Others realize that the dangers of inhaling are not worth the risk.

Giving up solvents

The good news about giving up solvents is that solvents are not **addictive**. People who are addicted to alcohol or **heroin** go through a long period of **withdrawal** when they stop. But as soon as someone stops using solvents they usually feel better, not worse. They have fewer headaches, their skin improves and they have more energy. Most of the damage to the nose, throat and lungs quickly heals. However, if the person has inhaled very poisonous substances, such as lead, there may be some permanent damage (see page 15).

Mental addiction

Inhaling solvents can be **psychologically addictive** for some people. When they stop, they miss the excitement and the **high**. Most people who inhale regularly do so because of other problems in their lives. When they stop inhaling the problems are still there. They may need help to solve them.

Did you know?

Spraying **aerosols** straight into the mouth is one of the most dangerous ways to inhale. Apart from possibly causing heart failure, the spray contains other things, such as solid particles of paint or lacquer, which can coat the throat and clog the lungs.

It is easy to give up using solvents. The body does not need them and the person feels physically better without them.

Saying no

Most people say no

Most people have never **inhaled** solvents. In Australia a survey found that only four people in any random group of a hundred people had tried solvents.

Knowing your own mind

What would you do if someone wants you to inhale with them? Many children are worried that if they say no, people will think they are scared or childish. However, it is dangerous to inhale solvents. It's not worth taking risks, just to appear cool.

You don't have to give an excuse for saying no. If you don't want to inhale, then just say so clearly. People are more likely to try to persuade you if they sense that you are unsure.

The best friends for you are those who accept you as you are and do not try to make you do anything you don't want to.

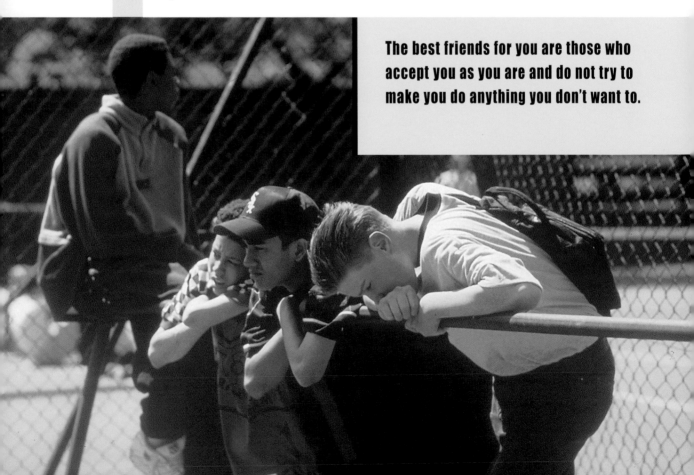

Best friends

As you grow up, you become more independent of your family. Being in a group with your friends can then seem very important. But if your friends are experimenting with solvents or other things that you don't want to do, then you should think about whether they are the right friends for you. Choose friends you like and who have the same interests as you.

When you do some form of exercise, your brain releases chemicals that make you feel good. Playing sport and exercising can give you a better 'buzz' than inhaling solvents or taking drugs.

What to say

If a best friend tried to persuade you to inhale solvents what would you say to them? How many reasons can you think of for saying no?

Did you know?

Most people say no to solvent abuse. In British secondary schools over 94% of students have not tried solvents. In Australia about 75% of secondary school students have never used solvents.

Avoiding difficult situations

Make an excuse

Try to avoid situations where you might be expected to **inhale** when you do not want to. Many young people like to spend time with their friends after school. But if you think your friends are planning to inhale, it is better to find an excuse not to go with them, than to go and then try to avoid inhaling.

Dangerous places

Be particularly wary if your friends go to an isolated and derelict place to inhale, or to a park or somewhere that may be safe during the day but is dangerous after dark. Many **drug dealers** and **addicts** use such places too. If anything goes wrong, it is much harder to get help. Nearly a third of deaths due to inhaling happen in a public place such as a park.

People who inhale often play truant. As a result, they don't just miss school work – they usually end up feeling bored and often get into trouble.

Truancy

People who inhale regularly often play truant from school and get involved in vandalism or fights. So hanging out with friends who are inhaling, even if you do not inhale yourself, means that you are also likely to get involved in other trouble.

Who is most at risk?

About seven out of every eight deaths due to solvents are boys. Why do you think more boys die from inhaling solvents than girls? There are usually fewer deaths in Britain during the winter than in the summer. Why do you think this is so?

Most schools have after-school activities that you can take part in. You might make some new friends as well.

Dealing with stress

Good and bad times

Growing up is an exciting and enjoyable time. You can try out new things and begin to make decisions for yourself. It can also be a difficult time. There are important exams that you have to work hard for. Friendships with your own sex and the opposite sex won't always run smoothly. Most people worry about the way they look, whether people will like them and what they are going to do with their lives.

Time to relax

When you are under stress, it is important to make time to relax and enjoy yourself. People who are working for exams do better if they take some time to do some physical exercise and relax their minds. Exercise helps to make you feel good.

Talking over a problem can help you feel better or help you to find a soloution. If you can't talk to a friend or someone in your family, talk to an adult you can trust, such as a teacher.

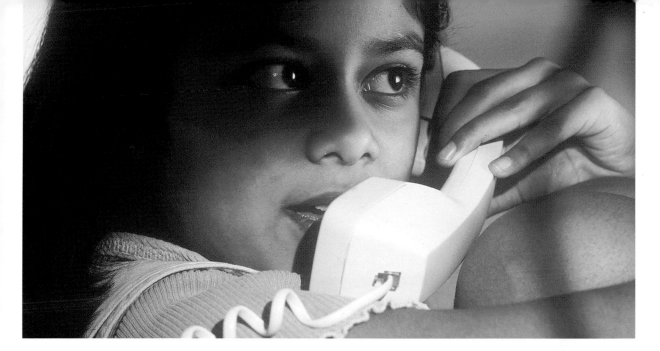

Getting help

Some young people have serious problems at home or at school. **Inhaling** may help them to escape from their problems, but only for a short time. When the effect of the solvent wears off the problems are still there and they feel tired and ill as well.

It is better to face up to problems and try to sort them out. If you have problems that you feel you cannot deal with, don't despair. Ask for help. There are people and organizations who can help you. If you can, ask for help from your family, your friends or your teachers. If at first people don't listen to you, go on looking and asking for help until you get it.

Sometimes talking on the telephone is easier than talking to someone face to face. If you can't talk to any of the people you know, then you can call Re-Solv or Childline.

Did you know?

If you want to talk to someone about solvent abuse, you can ring Re-Solv on their freephone helpline 0808 800 2345.

Childline is an organization in Britain that provides help and support for children and young people in trouble or in danger. Their freephone number is 0800 1111.

Talk it over

When you are unhappy it is easy to think that things will never change for the better. How would you persuade someone to get help with their problems?

Preventing solvent abuse

Not for sale

Inhaling solvents is so dangerous that many people want the government to prevent it. The law already says that shopkeepers must not sell products containing solvents if they think that a young person is going to inhale them – but how is a shopkeeper to know? In some shops, glues and other popular inhalants are kept behind the counter, but so many products contain solvents that it is impossible to keep them all out of reach.

Safer sprays

Sniffing aerosols is the most dangerous form of inhaling. Some people asked manufacturers to add an unpleasant smell to their aerosols. The manufacturers were unable to because no one would want to buy hairspray or deodorant that smelt terrible. However, many products which are sold as aerosols could be changed to sprays that work without a dangerous aerosol **propellant**.

Many substances can be sold as sprays that do not contain inhalants.

Beating the boredom

The best way to prevent people using solvents is to look at the reasons why they do it. Young people often feel bored and angry. They need to have places to go where they can do interesting and exciting things, such as acting in a play, performing in a band or learning how to rock-climb. Activities like these can help young people to feel more confident and more able to find a job in the future.

One way to prevent solvent abuse is to tackle the reasons why people do it. Young people often have nowhere to go and nothing they can afford to do. They need places, like this climbing wall, where they can meet and enjoy themselves without spending a lot of money.

Should the government take action?

What do you think the government should do to stop people abusing solvents? Think about how much money each of your suggestions would cost.

Useful contacts

Solvents

ADFAM National – offers confidential support and information to families and friends of drug users:
telephone: 020 7929 8900.

Australian Drug foundation – for information, write to:
409 King Street, Melbourne 3000
or telephone: Australia 03 9278 8100
or website: www.adf.org.au

Childline – provides free support for children or young people in trouble or danger:
freephone helpline: 0800 1111.

Direct Line – for counselling:
telephone: Australia 1800 136 385

Drugs in School – for advice and support concerning a drug incident in school:
freephone helpline: 0808 8000 800
open Monday-Friday 10.00 am to 5.00 pm.

Drug info Line –
telephone: Victoria 131570 or NSW 02 93612111

The National Drugs helpline – for helpful and friendly advice:
freephone helpline: 0800 77 66 00.

Release – 24-hour confidential helpline offering legal advice concerning arrest on drug charges and other drug matters:
telephone: 020 7603 8654.

Re-Solv – for information and support concerning solvent abuse:
freephone helpline: 0808 800 2345
open Monday-Friday 9.00am to 5.00 pm.

Glossary

addict someone who cannot give up a habit, such as smoking cigarettes or taking heroin

addictive causing someone to form a habit they cannot give up

aerosol a can containing a liquid which is released as a fine spray

asthma tightening of the tubes in the lungs which makes breathing difficult

butane a gas made from petrol and burnt as a fuel

cannabis an illegal drug made from hemp. Cannabis is also called marijuana and hashish.

cells the building blocks of all living things, including the human body

charged accused by the police

chemical a substance that is used in chemistry

depressant a substance that slows down the body's reactions and relaxes the muscles

drug dealer someone who sells or deals in drugs

Ecstasy an illegal stimulant

evaporate turn from a liquid into a gas

fumes unpleasant or poisonous gases or smoke

hallucinate to experience things that are imagined as if they are real

hallucinogen a substance that causes a person to hallucinate

heroin an addictive, illegal drug made from a particular kind of poppy

high drunk or exhilarated by drugs

illegal drug a drug, such as heroin, LSD or cannabis, which is forbidden by law

inhale breathe in

legal drug a substance which affects the body but is allowed by law. Medicines, coffee and tea are legal drugs.

LSD an illegal, powerful hallucinogen

medicine substance which is used to treat or cure illnesses

overdose too big a dose. An overdose of a drug can lead to unconsciousness or death.

physically addictive causing the body to be unable to work normally without a particular substance, such as nicotine in tobacco, or heroin

prescribed given a medicine under the advice or order of a doctor

propellant gas used in an aerosol to push a fine spray of the contents out of the can

psychologically addictive causing a person's behaviour to become dependent on using a particular substance. The person feels they cannot manage without it.

sniffing inhaling a solvent or volatile substance

solvent a liquid in which another substance is dissolved

stimulant a substance that speeds up the body

suffocate make unable to breathe

unconscious unaware of what is happening

vapour gas

volatile substance a substance that evaporates easily

withdrawal taking away, especially of an addictive drug. Withdrawal symptoms include craving and physically unpleasant feelings which are experienced until the body gets used to managing without the drug.

Index